human 𝄞 *c.*

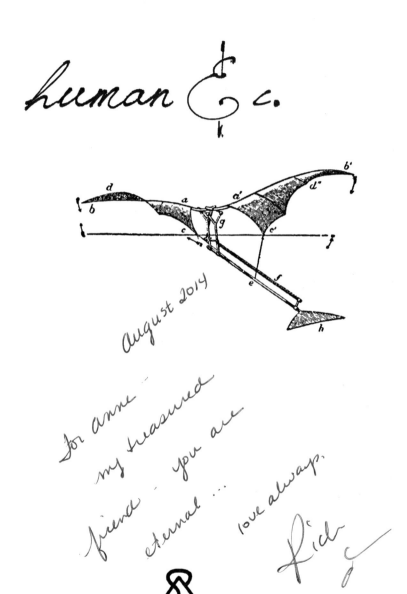

August 2014

for anne : my treasured
friend · you are
eternal ... love always,

Rich

NeoPoiesis Press, LLC

NeoPoiesis Press

Inquiries:
P.O. Box 38037
Houston, TX 77238-8037

Primary Address:
2775 Harbor Ave SW, Suite D
Seattle, WA 98126-2138

www.neopoiesispress.com

rich follett –human &c.
ISBN 978-0-9855577-8-2 (paperback : alk. paper)
         1. Poetry. I. Follett, Rich

Printed in the United States of America.

First Edition

To the human spirit, seeking always to rise above;
victorious only in falling to rise again ...

contents

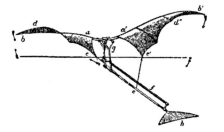

*kabaowek**

it began
that sweltering summer
(my sixth)
when i formed an ineluctable notion
to hurdle the rusting backyard swing set which
had always failed to provide
the flight that called from my bones.

my approach was feckless,
a fey wraith
etching wan, mincing curlicues
in the mocking sand;
yet, as i hurled my willow frame skyward,
i felt unseen arms bear me
to miraculous apogee
as i cleared the oxidized crossbar —
belying chronic asthma
with a warrior whoop.

mama,
watching in waspish horror
from our kitchen window,
wailed in anticipation of
my certain demise;
later, the tortured
'*o*'
of her contorted mask
would be my only referent
in accepting that levitation
had actually happened.

for the briefest moment,
as i descended,
as my pallid feet
ceased their panic-pedal

and rejoiced in regaining *terra firma*,
i saw them differently;
brown and bathed in
sacred dust
from the earth their mother
(the implausibility of this
did not register then;
does not register now).

shortly after
this dædalean endeavor,
the dream-loop began:

i am six,
as i was
on that long island summer day
long ago;
the swing set looms
as it did then
but the feet in the dream
are fleet –
are brown –
are ... mine?

running barefoot over white dunes
with a wind of my own creation
rushing in my ears,
blowing dried pine needles aside,
my drum heart pounding a primal beat
to drive the tattoo of my stride,
i leap ...
and my leap becomes true flight.

arms sprout pied down as i rise;
over the pipe
beyond the swing set
beyond the backyard

onto the mainland
north to the mountains
i fly;
the fullness and strength of my feathers
increasing with altitude and speed until
i am miles above our mother –
transformed into
an eagle,
carried aloft on echoes of ancestral song.

rivers run red
as i pass over;
my winged shadow far below
is dark and rich with freedom
and the promise of the hunt.

at day's end, sated, i return,
leaving air and aerie behind
until the dream comes anew
and ancient winds call forth my spirit wings.

these mid-life days,
i run less; dream less;
my feet are once again unsure and pale;
still, on stifling summer nights,
i am beckoned
back to white sand,
brown needles,
blue sky and remembered flight.

there was another summer
(my twelfth)
when a shinnecock caretaker
at the local game farm
(whose dog was half wolf)
showed me an eagle in a cage;
he said only

that it had been wounded and
never again would fly.

'he *remembers*'
i said;
'and he *dreams.*'

the indian did not reply;
instead, he listened as i told him of
the swing set, spirit wings and
rich, dark shadows ...

he regarded me silently, deeply;
a look of forever and of longing –
then *kabaowek* cried
and a single dappled feather
fluttered to the ground,
its quill at our feet.

i had no breath.

he reached down,
grasped the prize
and handed me ...
flight.

within,
rivers ran red.

these days,
these mid-life days,
the dream still comes;
the river below
runs red as i pass
(though my shadow is
cast by the moon).

later,
awake,
i run to the dresser,
open a sheltering drawer and
take up my totem feather –
now grown white
with years.

*algonquian, 'locked up.'

icarus speaks

sun above

sea below

one possible end

o irony

this moment alone

to learn

the death spiral

our one

true flight

tsunami/origami

helpless

in the wake of

the great wave

slowly

carefully

i fold in upon myself

one corner at a time

until

at last

i am a paper crane

winging east

to the rising sun

i fly in peace

my spirit

singing with hope

for tomorrow ...

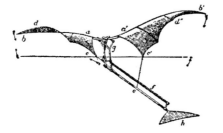

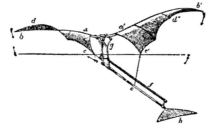

cinderella, deconstructed

she walked into the bar
and he did not look at her.

at first he seemed, to her, a footnote —
a human etcetera —
until the reality registered:
he did not *look* at her.

she was as she had always been;
sashaying, swaying,
sleek and slim-hipped in the little black dress of legend —
an ephemeral, pheromonal enchantress
with a panther's predatory precision.

he was inexplicably aloof.

from the moment she realized
he was indifferent,
he became the sole object of her desire:
she began a relentless, externally imperceptible implosion.

lowering herself to flirtation,
she freshened her luscious lipstick,
feigned inexperience,
projected an air of prurient innocence
and (this was her *pièce de résistance*) pouted.

for fifty feet in every direction,
fully formed adult males
became puerile, panting pinheads
throbbing and drooling untidily,
scenting conquest —

he alone was unfazed.
having no referent for diffidence,

she became centrifugally desperate;
a frantic, antic moth to his frore flame.

as midnight approached,
she exhausted the lexicon of known feminine wiles
in pursuit of his faintest apperception;

when at last he looked up,
he looked past her —
he did not look *at* her.

at one minute before midnight
she, lurid in her lust and bereft of reason,
deftly executed the last step of the dance of the seven veils with
wild abandon
and threw herself prostrate and quivering before him.

as a barful of sweating barbarians erupted in ecstatic paroxysms,
he looked at his watch;
he did not look at *her*.

disgraced, defeated and devastated,
she ran shrieking from the bar.

months later,
dressed like a scullery maid,
she was folding her laundry
at duds-n-suds
when the little black dress of legend appeared unbidden
between two dish towels.

bemused by the folly of her former self,
she snickered wryly
and allowed the barren garment to fall in a heap
on the pockmarked tile.

a quiet, gentle man

picked it up and handed it to her;
she did not look at him but
(sensing his warm and admiring gaze)
murmured embarrassed thanks
and began a casual conversation to mask the awkward moment.

through six washloads their dialogue continued,
ranging from the everyday to the existential —
he said "i like the way you think";
she said "i feel as if i know you."

at one minute before midnight
she finished folding her laundry and (at last) looked at him.

this time
he did not look at his watch —
he looked only at her.

they lived happily ever after.

duh.

clara

s
he
wan
ted a
modest
alabaster
obelisk so
me two feet
in height; ne
ither insignif
icant nor osten
tatious; set on a
simple base and
vined with piquant
sculpted ivy on a fili
gree trellis lifting sw
eet words of grateful
remembrance to wait
ing heaven. a reason
able request, she thought,
in light of a lifetime spent
thinking only of others, giv
ing endlessly and uncondit
ionally, without complaint.
to rest under an artful spire,
reflection in minimus of her
heart's secret cathedral, would
be a most fitting denouement.
she made her wishes known
to her husband, later lost at
sea in a pointless and ironically
tragicomic polar exploration in
volving ice floes, an albatross
and a badly corroded compass;
she also expressed her wishes
in painstaking detail to her six
children, each of whom appeared
to be reverent and rapt and each of
whom promptly went back to his
or her monumentally self-absorbed
excuse for not living productively.
upon her inconvenient demise, it was
decided for the sake of economy and
expediency to install a respectable
BLOCK OF NEW ENGLAND GRANITE,
PRACTICAL AND UNIFORM, WITH A
LL OF THE REQUIRED INFORMATION
SET IN NEAT ROWS OF DIGNIFIED, M
ASCULINE BLOCK LETTERS IDENTIC
AL TO THOSE ON THE OTHER STONE
ES SET IN NEAT ROWS THROUGHOU
T THE MEMORIAL PARK. YEARS FRO
M NOW, ONE OF HER GREAT - GREAT
GRANDCHILDREN, A GENEALOGIST,
WILL STOP BY FOR A MOMENT TO M
AKE NOTES AND TO PONDER THE HE
ARTLESS AMBIVALENCE OF DEATH.

epic

three booths down
at the chinese buffet
sat beowulf.

hair, flaxen;
skin, corrugated;
eyes, cerulean (flecked with brine);
his essence imposing, burnished, severe and commanding
(even when hunched over crab legs).

an anglo-saxon warrior in t-shirt and jeans;
out of place and time,
apparition and archetype all at once —
corporeal string theory and living literature
materialized in a single skipped heartbeat.

not so much sculpted as hewn,
his bulk and heft evinced
snapping sinew and cataclysmic combat —
an image borne not of aerobics and évian
but by preternatural victories wrenched from the maw of doom.

his aspect, wholly planes and angles;
nothing more than straight lines required
for authentic rendering.

i, not given to staring, stared.

simultaneously emasculated and vindicated,
comparatively effete,
(having fought only to bring words to life),
with chopsticks breathlessly poised over cooling chow fun,
i vainly sought plausible justifications — social survival strategies —

should he interrupt his gnawing
to return my admiring gaze.

after a long while,
he rose to return to the feast table —
towering, immutable,
mythic in his gait;
striding purposefully across the ages
to plunder and devour.

as i regarded with awe the fluid sinews
of a bronzed, scarred forearm —
as he deftly severed the claws of steamed sea monsters —
the long-abandoned herot of my imagination regained its hero
and i became the anonymous scylding scop
heralding hrothgar's legacy for the ages.

toying coyly with a limp rice noodle,
i was pondering immortality when
azure eyes met mine,
glowered
and dismissed my
envious intelligence.

time folded, suspended
as he grunted primordial awareness —
then resumed
gorging on grendel.

desktop thaumaturgy

a paper clip,
discarded casually;
casualty
of routine operations.

processing administrivia:
removing the woebegone wire, i am
exchanging inanities with a co-worker
when (in mid-sentence)
i blandly cast
the misbegotten miniature grapnel
aside.

a graceful arc;
a glimmer of suspended animation
and then
(inconceivably)
impertinent,
indomitable,
insouciant,
the coquettish coil comes to rest
in flagrante delicto —
coyly cantilevered
on its own rounded edge.

time stands still;

drawing in breath,
dimly aware of divine mystery,
i, bug-eyed and breathless,
whisper to my colleague,

"you saw that, right?"

mutual synaptic anarchy:
what were the chances?

in the nanosecond
between cognition and comprehension
the higgs boson is confirmed,
cancer is cured and
peace pervades the middle east;

for one gleaming arthurian moment,
anything is possible.

one frame later,
in epic synchronicity,
my colleague and i
(succumbing to
primordial hunter-gatherer dna and
envisioning youtube immortality)
lunge for cell-phone cameras.

stop-action, slow motion danse macabre;
infinitesimal seismic armageddon ensues —

elbows connect;
the mythic minimus
capsizes as

monday's mundane mantle
once again
descends ...

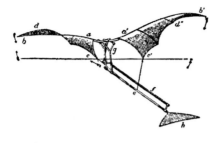

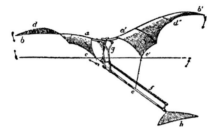

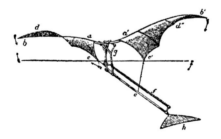

alum, lime, and time

two pickles
in a mason jar --
shenandoah dill,
grass-green and crisp;
wrinkled viridian jewels
inveigling
clear through
the closed door
of the refrigerator.

no side dishes, these;
rather, transcendent
bonnes bouches of brine --
each a petite paean
to halcyon summer.

one week ago,
the jar was full --
gift from a friend's kitchen;
the work of her loving hands.

in the time since,
my wife and i
(with childish grins
and dripping chins)
have savored each one so fully
as to have numbered and named them
with our delight;
thanks-praying for these benisons
(as dear to us as fleeting youth) and
repenting our reckless pickle lust
even as we reached
with giggling, guilty fingers
for another ...

one week ago,
the jar was full;
one week ago
the vibrant,
extraordinary young woman who
blessed us with
sunshine from a crock
was at our door --
today,
news of her passing.

incomprehensible, really,
that two pickles
in a mason jar
could be
all that remains --
the only tangible remnant
of her sweetness
in our life;
it is
so inexpressibly cruel
for the line between
here and gone
to be so fine,
the parting
so sudden.

here in our kitchen,
i stand in my bathrobe
feeling a chill
clear through
the closed door
of the refrigerator.

one week ago,
i would not have believed:
tonight

i open the refrigerator door
just to stare at
two pickles
in a mason jar
(two perfect, beryl lobes);
open the door,
hold my breath
and pray --
hoping against hope
that i will see them begin
to beat.

surety

late july neo-genesis:
yesterday, sun scorched, nut brown earth shards;
today, in profusion,
lycoris squamigera —
resurrection lily.

three months ago,
malachite strap leaves adorned this parchment plot;
with the solstice,
they became forgotten, dessicated tendrils
scattered by winds of dying spring.

now, against all reason, a roseate nosegay —
borne aloft on pencil-thin petioles
(daintily defying the drying dust of shenandoah midsummer).

any of the town's walnut women —
birdlike, pruned nonagenarian relicts —
will divulge with twinkling obsidian eyes that these miracle flowers
are more commonly called 'naked ladies',
recalling in the same breath
(with anachronistic maiden flush)
genteel archaic terms —
veranda; julep; gentleman caller.

if, with their airy florid terpsichore,
these seraphic heralds of autumn
can revivify parched earth and wizened crones,
zion
still waits …

wizening

raking leaves
late one autumn afternoon,

her shriveled hands
diminished twin replicants of
the rust-dotted implement
she wields,

ruhamah

with measured strokes

mitigates impending dissolution
beneath an ancient oak -

the one true
companion
her life has known.

how long they have danced
(oak and crone)
through growth and decline
is nearly as remarkable as

this rhythm
only they can know:

the secret,
scything sway
of years --

of sighs.

tree and trustee,

mirroring
psychic dessication;

wardens, they --
one with bark,
the other, parchment
stretched over bones which
ache to recall some purpose.

for today,
amid the petty entropy of
autumnal swirl,

gaia's cyclopic emerald
lawn-eye
remains open ...

exordium

she wore
her hair
in one long braid,
wound around
the top of her head
until it became
an alabaster pillbox —
prim standard
of her unwavering
propriety.

she was neither
oblivious to
its effect
upon her pupils
nor deterred by
our unruly gibes —
in the end,
the pillbox prevailed
(so it continued
through april --
we flouted
every primer,
learning nothing).

six a.m.
one bright may morning,
early to school,
i padded mischievously
down the asbestos corridor
to peer in
at her classroom door;
puckish surprise
my puerile aim.

inside,
she sat –
a septuagenarian sylph
serenely brushing
six feet of
undulating alban
gossamer.

i remember
weightlessness,
reverie,
light
and music;
nothing in
nine years
on earth
had prepared me
for such
ineffable
radiance.

i stood
transfixed;
one glorious moment
in dian's presence
before backing away
with shame
hissing
in every cilia.

later,
her immaculate cataract
restored to
pristine cylindrical obeisance,
she expounded upon
the virtues of cursive
and made perfect

chalk spirals
to inspire
fit chirography.

having *seen* her,
i scribbled stupidly
and dreamed of
wings ...

i knew

i knew
even as i ascended the stairs,
carrying her dinner on a filigree tray:
it was over.

fifteen is so young to know
but i did know —

and so did she.
her life was measured in giving;
so much
for so long
to so many
that we
who received her
selfless abundance
had long since abandoned
outward shows of gratitude

(we were not above thanks; rather,
she was embarrassed by
the merest morsel of appreciation) —

she existed solely to give;
we learned that accepting
was the kindest recompense.

she gave us sundays
around an ancient multifoliate mahogany table

on creaking, faux medieval
red-seated crackled pigskin chairs
(grandfather's was the only one with arms);

she gave us food beyond imagining —
perpetually overcooked;
each course gray and lifeless
yet somehow ambrosial —
served between snippets of
minced methodist hymn

(grandmother could neither cook nor sing
but paid no heed to destiny
in pursuing her passions).
she gave us a place at the table —
a place to rise above our shared dna.

she gave us
ourselves.

it was because she had given so much
that i knew
it was over
when she asked me to feed her.

one paper-thin, velvet touch of her furrowed hand
on my anguished cheek
heralded her obsequy:

'lambie, would you…?'
lambie would;

lambie did;

knowing full well
what it meant —
what it took for her to ask.

an elegy in applesauce;
one teaspoon, just level —

tissue-thin lips on generations-old silver,
a glimmer of rheumy, empathic understanding;
a flicker behind the cataracts
and then

for one terrible, beautiful moment
i glimpsed the universe of pain
from which her infinite gifts had sprung.

a delicate, labored swallow;
the rustle of lilac curls on crisp linen;

i remember
(or perhaps only wished for)
her featherlight kiss on my fretful brow
as i leaned in to say goodnight.

i knew
even as i descended the stairs,
carrying her dinner on a filigree tray:

it was over.

fifteen is so young to know

but i did know —

and so did she.

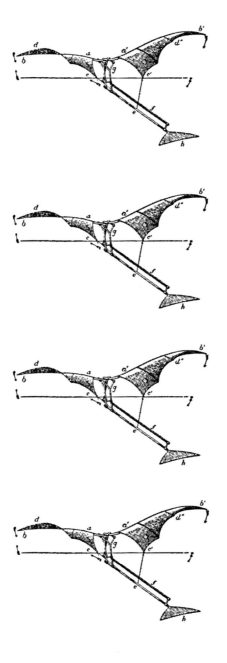

punchinello's last gloaming

the particular ways
in which we forget
    to see
        to cherish
        to remember

the particular days
in which we fly
    only
        to
           fall…

the particular haze
in which we flaunt
    our
        umbrageous
           myopia

the particular maze
in which we forswear
    absolution
        for
           all…

the particular praise
through which human frailty
    reveals

    amour-
           propre

these amaranthine roundelays
        each
           a death

without dying,

must not define
what art we find –

o, yet there is time:

rise;

    listen...

        see ...

barbed mirror

~ upon Henry Taylor's *Barbed Wire*, from *The Flying Change* (1986) ~

i existed, imprimis, to be a horse -
to define the pastorale for passers by;
my function, to feed and be fleet

to unfetter fancies for the earthbound
as i floated along the fenceline;
my grace god-given, my place primordial

with each of my merest movements,
(masterpieces of sublime fluidity), i
flustered the old men into dim longing,
their shame-bound, tobacco-stained hisses
echoing the remembered hitch in their loins
on summer nights a haggard generation removed from
the stagnant swelter of this, my dying day

it was an unexpected whinny on the wind, perhaps: a neigh; a
nicker;
far off, a filly or foal gamboling in the wanton apricot aura of
afternoon;
or, possibly, the careless clash of man and machine; some aimless,
nameless noise -

i was grazing, gazing at the men with leaf-brown faces
when some glimmer of
gut-wrenching ingrained genetic detritus
spurred me to wild, consanguine flight

my winged hooves against my will,
i was racing, raking along rows of stannic briars;
garroted as green grass ran red -
as the old men's leathery laughter lashed me on to oblivion

with the hemic buzz of my silvered slaughter
hung in the air like rustling sheaves,
i lowered my head to reproach their gaping faces;
the shriveling, tractor-plowed masks of those drying, dying men —
they who in a lifetime of barren labor had known but a moment's
grace
in the frenzied grip of perfidious procreation

it was then

in that mirrored moment

when at last

i flew...

nine eleven

the towers fell;

we

did not.

America

still sings:

chords of

courage,

strains of

hope

ring true.

years later,

i marvel at

leaves of grass

springing from

the fecund rubble of

dreams

that did not die.

America

still sings -

(lilac will

sweetly scent

dooryards

many millennia

hence).

the towers fell;

we

did not.

terms of engagement

i. bleed

it is possible
to exsanguinate a spirit;
to eviscerate hope;
to evacuate eternity from behind the eyes

it is possible
for a soul to become exanimate
long before mortality —
to evanesce

(it is possible
to extinguish humanity
within as well as without) . . .

we who did not fight
we who did not see
we can hear the stories
we can witness the wounds but
we cannot staunch the bleeding -

it is not possible
to exhume innocence

ii. honor

it is possible
to outlast hell...

we who did not fight
we who did not see
we cannot understand what it is

to be honorably inhuman;

we cannot comprehend that,
once having done so,
it is not possible to fully return
to a thankless world

iii. heal

it is possible
now,
together -

we fight
we see
we bleed
we honor

we begin to understand

we give thanks

we write, and so
we heal -

it is possible.

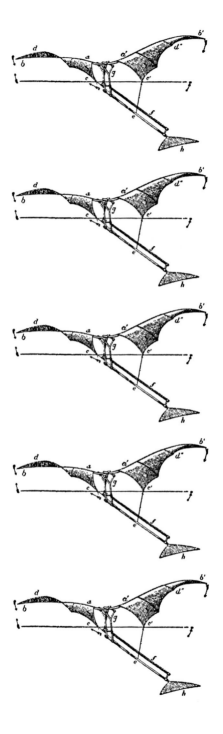

swētmete

oh,
i am weary of
dead
white men;

their voices dust-dry,
their verses
bleached bones of
desiccant truth
spewed from
aging, flaccid pens.

i crave

a
color
palate;

bloat and churn
for want of
prosodic zest.

soon
my griffonage will pass
into pantheons of
caucasian
faux-profundity;

in these
fatted, fetid days

what a valediction
any hint of
piquancy

would be ...

poetasters linger;
poet — tasters
are waiting to be born.

i want
to come to
the feast anew —

to sample
something
insouciantly spiced,
flung across the page
in cayenne profusion.

i long to ignite
my complacent gut
with fresh perspective.

oh,
i am wary of
dead
white men;

watching from
haughty
marble arches,
their arteries hardened --

cold

pallid

stone ...

Ποιέω (poiesis)

words
express least
what most needs saying:
poesy's heresy.

master?

mendicant?

words
do not signify –
age after age,
anguished odists spew
misanthropic monody.

perhaps
verisimilitude
in versification
is elegiac:
epics echo only to cithara;
lyrics, to lyre
(for want of barbitos,
ballads languish).

what if
apollo
(god of prophecy)
once decreed:
poetasters
are born
when pipes do not play?

prosodion
devolves to dithyramb;

order to entropy
for want of
accompanying airs.

what if,
in worshipping praxis,
we deny poiesis?

might
ars poetica
be not appolonian —
but, rather, dionysian?

tonight. a new *enkomion*:
a threnode to bacchus,
my paean
to pan ...

triage

today
my jubilee begins;
half a sentient century –
five decades extant,
sextant eyes
seeking event horizons ...

today
my jubilee begins;
i am surrounded by revelers
expecting a speech.

certainly
a marker is warranted;
some shred of sagacity
to eulogize youth
amidst encroaching nitre and rheum.

obligated by longevity;
resigned to the impossibility
of reprieve;
peering inward and
steering a poetic course;
returning to scylla and charybdis
armed with shards of battle-scarred outrage,
i steel my newly wizened, hoary spirit
for apocalyptic confrontation
only to discover
a child's laughter —
tintinnabulation from
armageddon's crater.

three truths reverberate:
i am *here,*

(far longer than i ever thought i would be);
i am *happy*
(far more than i ever thought i could be);
i am *hopeful*
(a mockery of reason, and yet . . .).

my thoughts now
are of daisies
in reckless profusion —
an ebullient garland
of undreamt tomorrows.

bereft of appropriate thanks,
i giddily chart a course toward home and
my well-meaning friends —
returning to their
jocular gibes and black balloon bouquets
with unprecedented equanimity.

today
my jubilee begins;
sagacity will have to wait
until the child
has finished singing.

plunge

~ co-write with Rachael Delamar (Rachael BytheSea) ~

i.

cold sweat on trembling skin;
trepidation's fetid breath
carries the kiss of death -
a falling, cursed life
waits to expire in
the downward spiral to follow.

no holding back, now;
the sacrifice of self
to endless air
is inevitable ...

terror below;
i am frozen -
movement exists only in memory.

i ponder:
how does one meet death?

pencil dive?

head first?

eyes open, mouth closed?

looking down,
pool-ripples are waves
violently surging; grinding;
sandblasting scars that will morph into
beach-glass polaroids of bright days long past -
the parachute of innocence

opens only to fail.

sudden serum;
an inoculation of adrenaline;
a saul drum heart beat as
junkie verse assails and visions take over.

giddy now; intoxicated;
the promise of warm, wet skin
tingles the top of my head, brushes the heart and
surges into fingertips -
as dread's incessant throb abates,
i s-l-o-w-l-y uncurl death-grip toes ...

discovering mettle, i leap effortlessly:
the world collapses at warped seams;
the drop flows into slow motion,
allowing me ample time
to memorize protracted scenery into garbled prose -
to swallow the barbiturate of bruising contact.

in my ardor for surrender
to this orgasmic plunge
i imagine i live my days
as fearlessly as poets write;
turning every opportunity into
a flawless dive off the high board -
the reality is
there is nothing to do after the leap
but twist and wait to hit the water.

daring here, doing now, thinking after;
discarding the fetal crouch;
diving high into the torrential downpour of
misspent tears -
misspent years -
i soar to swallow the days of fright.

ii.

impact.

aqueous visions end in a pool
of dust: a raging sandstorm.

the water is quicksand;
i, parched and gasping,
am no longer falling - i am sinking
into the shapeless, shifting void below
(terror is elemental,
whatever element we're in).

beneath the surface now,
living a lifetime in a nanosecond,
i return to the streets of my brokenness -
newly combative;
defying normalcy's dotted lines.

i run facing traffic,
stare down all smoldering eyes,
hellbent on becoming a slaughterer of timidity -
reckless in my lust to
outrace the taint of fear.

i am hyper-vigilant, indestructible:
my brain anticipates disasters
before, after;
sidewalks say 'closed'
so i proceed without reason,
following damned tracks through tsunamis
only to battle ghosts
(voids of vanishing breath).

i feel a phantom vibration:
a shivering harbinger of rank death,

shadowing, stalking -
i know all too well
i am walking
on my own grave.

i plunge, ever deeper...

under the quicksand's surface,
blind and hyperventilating,
i flail pell-mell;
retching
(reaching from below,
the wormy fingers of my own cowardice
clutch and claw
to claim their due).

nine feet under, i am still breathing.

as the bars of my death-prison lower,
i scratch and scream,
burning lungs taking in dank liquid earth,
taking on water ...

water ...?

iii.

cold water has a way
of shocking the system into action;
the will to survive
often mimics blasphemy.

my body has power -
my curves accentuate life,
mocking mortality.
i am rising, breaking through:

i am walking on water ...

overhead, the diving board
looks down haughtily;
my strokes are strong and
i find solid concrete -
cling to the edge.

the edge is not hard.

it is *soft*.

it is an heirloom quilt stitched by hand -
proof of life beyond death.

within, i am dry;

safe; warm;
what ghosts may come
will bring only welcome memories.

a new kind of shudder comes;
a motivating aftershock -
dive higher,
run faster,
live more ...

there is nothing to do after the leap
but twist and wait to hit the water.

consonance

for one moment
arm in arm,
gazing skyward
(who knew that stars could
actually form a canopy?)

for one heartbeat-optional moment
bathed in twinkling chastity
we lived wholly within each other,
you and i —
perfect friends,
god-given

for one resplendent,
montane midnight moment
we held
one breath
in two bodies
beneath orion
with philotes smiling down

for one unstained moment of divine grace,
twin exhaled awe-spirals danced
a november paean

for one immortal moment
(that one was enough)

agápe
was ours …

something there is (psalm)

something there is
about the spirit
that yearns to transcend
this earth we know

something that calls
(o can you hear it)
saying

come away

come fly

let go

if we leap
the net will be waiting

if we seek
it is written
we shall find

something there is
about the spirit
something human
and yet divine

some joys we know
live on forever
while some spiral downward
into dust

so we hold on to
the days we treasure

(their memory is
a sacred trust)

if we believe
eternity follows
we will weave our dreams
among the stars

something there is
about tomorrow
something promised
but not yet ours

sometimes we fly

sometimes we fall

sometimes we never get
off the ground
at all

but for all our human failings
despite our foolish pride
there's a spark of perfection
that cannot be denied

through our follies and
our foibles
(when all is
said and
done)
we live for love

we live
for love

something there is

about forgiveness
that sweetens and
sanctifies
our days

some wind
that lifts up
our voice

to heaven

to deepen and
magnify
our praise

it is through grace
that hope
springs eternal

if we have faith
then love
will
conquer
all

something there is
about compassion

eden's echo -

a distant call

Rich Follett is a High School English, Theatre, and Mythology teacher who has been writing poems and songs for more than 35 years. His poems have been featured in numerous online and print journals, including BlazeVox, Four Branches Press, The Montucky Review, Paraphilia, Exercise Bowler, Leaf Garden Press and CounterExample Poetics, for which he is a featured artist. He lives with his wife Mary Ruth Alred Follett in the Shenandoah Valley of Virginia, where he also pursues his interests as a professional actor, singer/songwriter, playwright and director.

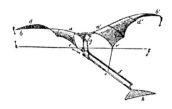

Alphonse Pénaud, born in Paris, France in 1850, believed wholeheartedly that it was possible (with vision, imagination and a set of man-made wings) for human beings to fly. He devoted his life to producing a series of toys — the graphic above and throughout this volume is of his *artificial bird* (ornithopter) from 1872 — and working models of flight devices, becoming along the way a member of the *Société Aéronautique de France* and ultimately serving as its Vice President.

In 1876, Pénaud worked with fellow *Société* member Paul Gauchot to design an amphibious monoplane with a retractable undercarriage. After failing to secure funding for his and Gauchot's visionary design, Pénaud sank into an emotional and psychological abyss, culminating in his untimely death by suicide in1880.

If only Pénaud could have known that, halfway across the world, Ohio farmer Milton Wright presented his sons Wilbur and Orville in 1878 with a handmade toy 'helicopter' based on Pénaud's designs! Later, the Wright brothers would cite this toy as one of their greatest inspirations in achieving what had long been considered impossible — human flight.

In words, in dreams and in visions, the opiate of flight still lulls and lures us all, spurring us on …

Alphonse Pénaud

1850 - 1880

The following journals have previously published poems
from this volume in print or online:

BlazeVox
Calliope Nerve
Connections Magazine (College of Southern Maryland)
CounterExample Poetics
Edgar and Lenore's Publishing House
Exercise Bowler
Four Branches Press
The Montucky Review
Sugar Mule

~ thanks and Godspeed ~

NeoPoiesis: *a new way of making*

1) in ancient Greece, poiesis referred to the process of making: creation - production - organization - formation - causation

2) a process that can be physical and spiritual, biological and intellectual, artistic and technological, material and teleological, efficient and formal

3) a means of modifying the environment and a method of organizing the self, the making of art and music and poetry, the fashioning of memory and history and philosophy, the construction of perception and expression and reality

4) an independent publisher with a steadfast goal to print and promote outstanding poets, writers and artists that reflect the creative drive and spirit of the new electronic landscape

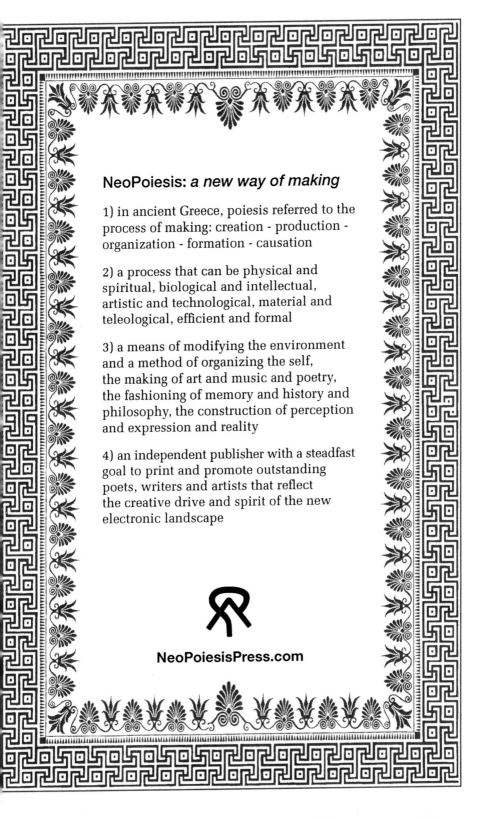

NeoPoiesisPress.com

CPSIA information can be obtained at www.ICGtesting.com
Printed in the USA
BVOW04s2142051113

335544BV00007B/42/P

9 780985 557782